THIS BOOK BELONGS TO:

_____

_____

Shop our other books at
www.sillyslothpress.com

For questions and customer service, email us at
support@sillyslothpress.com

JOKE 1

Q: WHY DO SOCCER PLAYERS DO SO WELL IN MATH?

A: THEY KNOW HOW TO USE THEIR HEADS!

JOKE 2

Q: HOW IS EDUCATION LIKE AN ERECTION?

A: IF YOU HAVE IT, IT SHOWS.

JOKE 3

Q: WHY DID THE BIOLOGY TEACHER NOT WATER ALL OF THE PLANTS?

A: BECAUSE HE COULDN'T FIND THE THYME.

JOKE 4

Q: WHAT IS THE PURPOSE OF TAKING HORRIBLE ELEMENTARY SCHOOL PICTURES?

A: IT'S SOCIETY'S WAY OF PREPARING YOU FOR YOUR DRIVER'S LICENSE PHOTO.

JOKE 5

Q: WHY DO PENCILS SHAVE?

A: TO LOOK SHARP.

JOKE 6

Q: WHAT'S THE DIFFERENCE BETWEEN A DOG AND A MARINE BIOLOGIST?

A: ONE WAGS ITS TAIL AND THE OTHER TAGS A WHALE.

JOKE 7

Q: DID YOU HEAR ABOUT THE ITALIAN CHEF WHO DIED?

A: HE PASTA WAY!

JOKE 8

Q: WHAT HAPPENED TO THE GEOMETRY TEACHER WHO LEFT HER PARROT'S COOP OPEN?

A: POLYGON.

JOKE 9

Q: WHY DID THE COMPUTER SCIENCE TEACHER QUIT?

A: HE LOST HIS DRIVE.

JOKE 10

Q: WHAT IS A PROOF?

A: ONE-HALF PERCENT OF ALCOHOL.

JOKE 11

Q: WHY DOES A MERMAID WEAR SEASHELLS?

A: BECAUSE SHE OUTGREW HER B-SHELLS!

JOKE 12

Q: WHAT WOULD HAPPEN IF YOU TOOK THE SCHOOL BUS HOME?

A: THE POLICE WOULD MAKE YOU BRING IT BACK.

JOKE 13

Q: WHAT DID THE ENGLISH TEACHER SAY WHEN TAKING THE CLASS PICTURE?

A: SIMILE!

JOKE 14

Q: WHY DIDN'T THE SUN GO TO COLLEGE?

A: IT ALREADY HAS A MILLION DEGREES.

JOKE 15

Q: WHAT IS A PHYSICIST'S FAVORITE FOOD?

A: FISSION CHIPS.

JOKE 16

Q: WHY DID THE STUDENT WEAR GLASSES IN MATH CLASS?

A: THEY IMPROVE DI-VISION.

JOKE 17

Q: WHY DID THE SOCIAL STUDIES TEACHER QUIT?

A: TEACHING HISTORY IS OLD NEWS.

JOKE 18

Q: WHAT'S THE LONGEST WORD IN THE DICTIONARY?

A: SMILES. BECAUSE THERE'S A MILE BETWEEN THE FIRST AND LAST LETTERS.

JOKE 19

Q: WHAT THREE BONES DO TEACHERS NEED?

A: WISH BONE, BACKBONE, FUNNY BONE.

JOKE 20

Q: WHY WAS THE PANDA KICKED OUT OF CHEMISTRY LAB?

A: BECAUSE HE CREATED PANDEMONIUM.

JOKE 21

Q: WHAT DO YOU GET WHEN YOU TAKE A COMPUTER ICE SKATING?

A: A SLIPPED DISK.

JOKE 22

Q: WHERE DO GALAXIES GO TO COLLEGE?

A: UNIVERSITY.

JOKE 23

Q: WHAT HORMONES DOES A SHARK USE TO SWIM INSIDE A HOUSE?

A: INDOOR FINS.

JOKE 24

Q: DID YOU HEAR ABOUT THE MATH STUDENT WHO FEARS NEGATIVE NUMBERS?

A: HE WILL STOP AT NOTHING TO AVOID THEM.

JOKE 25

Q: WHY WAS THE MATH TEACHER ARRESTED?

A: FOR PLOTTING WEAPONS OF MATH INSTRUCTION.

JOKE 26

Q: TEACHER: "IF YOUR DAD EARNED $800 A WEEK AND GAVE YOUR MOM HALF, WHAT WOULD SHE HAVE?"

A: STUDENT: "A HEART ATTACK."

JOKE 27

Q: WHY DID THE GIRL EAT HER HOMEWORK?

A: BECAUSE SHE DIDN'T HAVE A DOG.

JOKE 28

Q: WHO IS EVERYONE'S BEST FRIEND ON THE FIRST DAY OF SCHOOL?

A: THEIR PRINCI-PAL.

JOKE 29

Q: WHAT IS THE GREAT DEPRESSION?

A: SPENDING MORE MONEY ON SCHOOL SUPPLIES THAN YOUR WARDROBE.

JOKE 30

Q: WHY IS GUM BAD AT MATH?

A: IT ALWAYS GETS STUCK ON PROBLEMS.

JOKE 31

Q: WHAT IS THE DIFFERENCE BETWEEN A SCHOOL BUS AND A PORCUPINE?

A: A PORCUPINE KEEPS THE LITTLE PRICKS ON THE OUTSIDE.

JOKE 32

Q: WHY DID MICHAEL'S GRADES DROP AFTER THE HOLIDAYS?

A: BECAUSE EVERYTHING WAS MARKED DOWN!

JOKE 33

Q: WHAT U.S. STATE HAS THE MOST MATH TEACHERS?

A: MATHACHUSSETS.

JOKE 34

Q: HOW DO TREES USE THE COMPUTER?

A: THEY LOG ON!

JOKE 35

Q: WHAT IS AN ENGLISH TEACHER'S FAVORITE DESSERT?

A: SYNONYM ROLLS.

JOKE 36

Q: WHAT'S WHITE WHEN IT'S DIRTY AND BLACK WHEN IT'S CLEAN?

A: A BLACKBOARD.

JOKE 37

Q: WHY IS CORN THE BEST LISTENER?

A: IT'S ALL EARS.

JOKE 38

Q: WHY DO MELONS HAVE WEDDINGS?

A: BECAUSE THEY CANTALOUPE!

JOKE 39

Q: WHAT DO YOU CALL A PONY WITH A COUGH?

A: A LITTLE HORSE!

JOKE 40

Q: WHY DID THE STUDENT FAIL HER ART EXAM?

A: BY USING THE WRONG PENCIL, IT JUST WASN'T 2B.

JOKE 41

Q: HOW CAN YOU TURN A DIME INTO 20 CENTS?

A: HOLD IT IN FRONT OF THE MIRROR.

JOKE 42

Q: WHAT WOULD BE A GREAT FUNDRAISER FOR SCHOOLS?

A: A CASH BAR ON PARENT/ TEACHER NIGHTS.

JOKE 43

Q: WHY DIDN'T THE TOILET PAPER CROSS THE ROAD?

A: IT GOT STUCK IN A CRACK.

JOKE 44

Q: WHY DON'T ENGLISH TEACHERS LIKE PAROLE?

A: THEY PREFER COMPLETE SENTENCES.

JOKE 45

Q: WHAT DID ARNOLD SCHWARZENEGGER SAY WHEN HE WAS INVITED TO A CLASSICAL MUSICIAN COSTUME PARTY?

A: I'LL BE BACH.

JOKE 46

Q: WHY DID THE SCARECROW RECEIVE A TROPHY?

A: HE WAS OUTSTANDING IN HIS FIELD!

JOKE 47

Q: WHY IS THE OBTUSE TRIANGLE ALWAYS SAD?

A: BECAUSE IT IS NEVER RIGHT.

JOKE 48

Q: WHY DID THE FIRST GRADER BRING A SPOON TO HER FIRST DAY OF SCHOOL?

A: SHE THOUGHT IT WAS SUNDAE SCHOOL.

JOKE 49

Q: WHAT DID ONE TRAFFIC LIGHT SAY TO THE OTHER?

A: STOP LOOKING! I AM CHANGING!

JOKE 50

Q: WHY DO TREES SEEM SUSPICIOUS ON SUNNY DAYS?

A: THEY JUST SEEM A LITTLE SHADY!

JOKE 51

Q: WHAT DID THE MATH BOOK SAY TO THE SCIENCE BOOK?

A: YOU CAN ALWAYS COUNT ON ME.

JOKE 52

Q: WHAT DO LIBRARIANS USE AS FISHING BAIT?

A: BOOKWORMS.

JOKE 53

Q: WHY DID THE STUDENTS EAT THEIR HOMEWORK?

A: BECAUSE THE TEACHER SAID THAT IT WAS A PIECE OF CAKE.

JOKE 54

Q: WHAT TYPE OF FLOWERS DOES EVERYBODY HAVE?

A: TWO-LIPS.

JOKE 61

Q: WHAT TYPE OF SCHOOL WOULD YOU SEE ON A MOUNTAIN TOP?

A: HEIGHTS SCHOOL.

JOKE 62

Q: WHAT IS THE DIFFERENCE BETWEEN A TEACHER AND A TRAIN?

A: A TEACHER SAYS, "SPIT OUT THE GUM!" A TRAIN SAYS, "CHEW! CHEW!"

JOKE 63

Q: WHY DID THE CHICKEN CROSS THE ROAD?

A: BECAUSE THE CHICKEN NEXT TO HIM WOULDN'T KEEP A 6-FOOT DISTANCE.

JOKE 64

Q: WHAT DO YOU CALL A RESTLESS NUMBER?

A: A ROAMIN' NUMERAL.

JOKE 65

Q: WHY DO CHEMISTRY TEACHERS LIKE TO LECTURE ABOUT AMMONIA?

A: BECAUSE IT'S BASIC KNOWLEDGE.

JOKE 66

Q: WHERE DO DOOR-MAKERS LEARN THEIR SKILL?

A: THE SCHOOL OF HARD KNOCKS.

JOKE 67

Q: WHY ARE HISTORY BOOKS LIKE FRUIT CAKES?

A: BECAUSE THEY'RE FULL OF DATES.

JOKE 68

Q: DID YOU HEAR WHAT HAPPENED TO THE MUSIC TEACHER WHO PLAYED THROUGH THE SILENT PART OF A SONG?

A: SHE WAS CHARGED WITH RESISTING A REST.

JOKE 69

Q: WHY DID THE BOY GO TO SCHOOL WITH HIS JEANS TUCKED INTO HIS SOCKS?

A: TO PROTECT HIMSELF FROM MATHEMA-TICKS.

JOKE 70

Q: WHY DID SANTA MAJOR IN MUSIC?

A: TO WORK ON HIS RAPPING SKILLS.

JOKE 71

Q: WHAT HAPPENED WHEN THE TEACHER ASKED THE CLASS A QUESTION?

A: THE STUDENTS WERE ALL UP IN ARMS.

JOKE 72

Q: WHAT DO YOU CALL AN ANT THAT HAS BEEN REJECTED BY SOCIETY?

A: A SOCIALLY DISSED ANT.

JOKE 73

Q: WHAT TYPE OF MEALS DO MATH TEACHERS EAT?

A: SQUARE ONES.

JOKE 74

Q: WHAT DO YOU LEARN AT WITCH SCHOOL?

A: SPELLING.

JOKE 75

Q: WHAT DO YOU DO WHEN NO ONE LAUGHS AT YOUR SCIENCE JOKES?

A: KEEP TRYING UNTIL YOU GET A REACTION.

JOKE 76

Q: WHY DID THE SCIENTIST GO TO THE TANNING SALON?

A: BECAUSE HE WAS A PALEONTOLOGIST.

JOKE 77

Q: WHY DID SEVEN EAT NINE?

A: BECAUSE YOU'RE SUPPOSED TO EAT 3 SQUARED MEALS A DAY!

JOKE 78

Q: WHY DID THE SKELETON SKIP PROM?

A: HE HAD NOBODY TO DANCE WITH.

JOKE 79

Q: WHY DIDN'T THE STUDENT TURN IN HIS ESSAY?

A: BECAUSE HE AIN'T NO SNITCH.

JOKE 80

Q: WHAT DO YOU GET WHEN YOU CROSS A TEACHER WITH A MOSQUITO?

A: BLOOD TESTS.

JOKE 81

Q: WHY WAS THERE THUNDER AND LIGHTNING IN THE LAB?

A: THE SCIENTISTS WERE BRAINSTORMING

JOKE 82

Q: WHY DID THE M&M APPLY FOR COLLEGE?

A: BECAUSE SHE WANTED TO BE A SMARTIE!

JOKE 83

Q: WHY WAS THE MUSIC CLASS CHAOTIC?

A: THE STUDENTS WERE ALL KEYED UP.

JOKE 84

Q: WHAT DOES LIFE HAVE IN COMMON WITH TOILET PAPER?

A: YOU'RE EITHER ON A ROLL OR TAKING SHIT FROM SOMEONE.

JOKE 85

Q: WHY DID THE TRIANGLE MAKE THE BASKETBALL TEAM OVER THE RECTANGLE?

A: HE ALWAYS MADE THREE-POINTERS.

JOKE 86

Q: WHAT DO YOU GET WHEN YOU CROSS A SNOWMAN WITH A VAMPIRE?

A: FROSTBITE.

JOKE 87

Q: WHY DID THE ATHEIST FAIL A MATH TEST ON EXPONENTIAL FUNCTIONS?

A: SHE DOESN'T BELIEVE IN HIGHER POWERS.

JOKE 88

Q: WHAT DO YOU CALL A PROGRAMMER FROM FINLAND?

A: NERDIC.

JOKE 89

Q: WHAT DO YOU CALL A GUY WITH A RUBBER TOE?

A: ROBERTO!

JOKE 90

Q: WHAT DO YOU CALL FRIENDS WHO LOVE MATH?

A: ALGEBROS.

JOKE 91

Q: WHAT IS A SNAKE'S FAVORITE SUBJECT?

A: HISSS-TORY

JOKE 92

Q: TEACHER: "YOU MISSED CLASS YESTERDAY, DIDN'T YOU?"

A: STUDENT: "NOT REALLY."

JOKE 93

Q: WHY WAS THE FIRST-GRADE TEACHER ARRESTED FOR DRUG POSSESSION?

A: THE SMALL PUPILS WERE A DEAD GIVEAWAY.

JOKE 94

Q: WHERE DO SURFERS GET EDUCATED?

A: BOARDING SCHOOL.

JOKE 95

Q: WHAT DO YOU CALL A HEN THAT CAN COUNT HER OWN EGGS?

A: A MATHAMACHICKEN!

JOKE 96

Q: WHAT IS A PERK OF BEING A MUSIC TEACHER?

A: YOU CAN YELL, "F, YOU GUYS!" WITHOUT CONSEQUENCE.

JOKE 97

Q: WHAT DO YOU CALL THE NUMBER 7 AND THE NUMBER 3 WHEN THEY GO OUT ON A DATE?

A: THE ODD COUPLE (BUT 7 IS IN HER PRIME).

JOKE 98

Q: HOW DO YOU KNOW SATURN HAS BEEN MARRIED BEFORE?

A: BECAUSE IT HAS A LOT OF RINGS.

JOKE 99

Q: WHY SHOULD YOU NEVER BELIEVE THE KING OF THE JUNGLE?

A: BECAUSE HE'S ALWAYS LION.

JOKE 100

Q: WHAT IS AN EXTREME SPORT FOR STUDENTS?

A: DOING THEIR HOMEWORK WHILE THE TEACHER IS COLLECTING IT.

JOKE 101

Q: HOW DO YOU SPELL HARD WATER WITH 3 LETTERS?

A: ICE!

JOKE 102

Q: WHY IS BEER NEVER SERVED AT A MATH PARTY?

A: BECAUSE DRINKING AND DERIVING IS ILLEGAL.

JOKE 103

Q: TEACHER: "I HOPE I DIDN'T SEE YOU LOOKING AT JILL'S EXAM?"

A: STUDENT: "I HOPE YOU DIDN'T EITHER."

JOKE 104

Q: WHY DID THE BEAR DISSOLVE IN WATER?

A: IT WAS POLAR.

JOKE 105

Q: DID YOU HEAR ABOUT THE POTATO THAT TEACHES MIDDLE SCHOOL?

A: HE'S ALWAYS DREAMED OF BEING AN EDU-TATER.

JOKE 106

Q: WHAT DO YOU CALL A WELL-
EDUCATED FARMER?

A: A FARMACIST.

JOKE 107

Q: WHAT WILL BE A
MANDATORY COURSE IN
20 YEARS?

A: EYE CONTACT.

JOKE 108

Q: DID YOU HEAR THE RUMOR
ABOUT BUTTER?

A: WELL, I'M NOT GOING TO
SPREAD IT!

JOKE 109

Q: WHAT TYPE OF BUS DOESN'T REQUIRE GAS?

A: A SYLLABUS.

JOKE 110

Q: WHAT DID THE LEFT BUTT CHEEK SAY TO THE RIGHT BUTT CHEEK?

A: TOGETHER, WE CAN STOP THIS CRAP.

JOKE 111

Q: WHAT DID THE PHYSICS TEACHER SAY TO THE STUDENT ABOUT TO JUMP OFF A BRIDGE?

A: "DON'T DO IT, YOU HAVE SO MUCH POTENTIAL."

JOKE 112

Q: HOW DID VIKINGS COMMUNICATE?

A: WITH NORSE CODE.

JOKE 113

Q: TEACHER: "WHAT IS IRONY?"

A: STUDENT: "IRONY IS WHEN SOMETHING HAS THE CHEMICAL SYMBOL FE."

JOKE 114

Q: WHAT DO YOU CALL AN ENGLISH PROFESSOR WITH A SOCIAL MEDIA ADDICTION?

A: AN INSTAGRAMMAR.

JOKE 115

Q: WHY SHOULD YOU SUPPORT BACTERIA?

A: THEY ARE THE ONLY CULTURE SOME PEOPLE HAVE.

JOKE 116

Q: WHAT'S A NINJA'S FAVORITE TYPE OF SHOES?

A: SNEAKERS!

JOKE 117

Q: WHY ARE GEOMETRY STUDENTS ALWAYS TIRED?

A: THEY ARE ALL OUT OF SHAPE.

JOKE 118

Q: WHAT DID THE CELL SAY WHEN IT WAS DIVIDING?

A: "IT'S NOT YOU, IT'S ME."

JOKE 119

Q: WHO'S THE KING OF THE CLASSROOM?

A: THE RULER.

JOKE 120

Q: WHAT DO MATHE-MATICIANS DO AFTER A SNOWSTORM?

A: MAKE SNOW ANGLES!

JOKE 121

Q: WHY WAS THE STUDENT'S FINAL EXAM ALL WET?

A: IT WAS BELOW C LEVEL.

JOKE 122

Q: WHY WAS THE ENGLISH TEACHER ARRESTED FOR VANDALISM?

A: SHE TRIED TO CORRECT A 'GOT MILK?' SIGN.

JOKE 123

Q: WHAT DO YOU CALL IT WHEN TWO ORCHESTRA STUDENTS FIGHT?

A: AN ACT OF VIOLINS.

JOKE 124

Q: WHAT IS THE TROUBLE FROM ONLY LEARNING FROM EXPERIENCE?

A: YOU NEVER GRADUATE.

JOKE 125

Q: WHAT'S A CHALK BOARD'S FAVORITE DRINK?

A: HOT CHALK-OLATE.

JOKE 126

Q: WHY ARE EDUCATED PEOPLE SO HOT?

A: THEY HAVE A LOT OF DEGREES.

JOKE 127

Q: WHY DID THE ECHO GET DETENTION?

A: FOR ANSWERING BACK.

JOKE 128

Q: WHY WAS THE EQUAL SIGN SO MODEST?

A: HE KNEW HE WASN'T GREATER THAN OR LESS THAN ANYONE ELSE.

JOKE 129

Q: HOW CAN YOU TELL THE DIFFERENCE BETWEEN A CHEMISTRY TEACHER AND A POLITICIAN?

A: ASK THEM TO PRONOUNCE THE WORD: UNIONIZED.

JOKE 130

Q: WHAT CAN A TEACHER SAY IN CLASS AND DURING SEX?

A: I BETTER WRAP THIS UP, OR YOU'LL MISS YOUR NEXT PERIOD.

JOKE 131

Q: WHY DID THE BROOM FAIL SCHOOL?

A: IT WAS ALWAYS SWEEPING DURING CLASS.

JOKE 132

Q: WHY WAS THE FOOTBALL COACH SCREAMING AT THE VENDING MACHINE?

A: HE WANTED HIS QUARTER BACK.

JOKE 133

Q: WHY WAS THE GYM TEACHER FIRED?

A: HE JUST DIDN'T WORK OUT.

JOKE 134

Q: WHAT DID THE FEMUR SAY TO THE PATELLA?

A: I KNEED YOU.

JOKE 135

Q: WHAT DO YOU CALL A TEACHER WITHOUT STUDENTS?

A: HAPPY.

JOKE 136

Q: WHY SHOULDN'T YOU TRUST A MATH TEACHER WITH GRAPH PAPER IN THEIR HANDS?

A: BECAUSE THEY'RE PLOTTING SOMETHING.

JOKE 137

Q: WHY DID THE TEACHER GO TO THE BEACH?

A: TO TEST THE WATER.

JOKE 138

Q: HOW IS A CHEMISTRY LAB SIMILAR TO A HOUSE PARTY?

A: SOME PEOPLE DROP ACID WHILE OTHERS DROP THE BASE.

JOKE 139

Q: WHAT IS GRAMMAR?

A: THE DIFFERENCE BETWEEN KNOWING YOUR SHIT, AND KNOWING YOU'RE SHIT.

JOKE 140

Q: HOW DO YOU KNOW THE MOON IS GOING BROKE?

A: IT'S DOWN TO ITS LAST QUARTER.

JOKE 141

Q: HOW CAN TEACHERS SAVE TIME DECORATING FOR ALL THE HOLIDAYS?

A: PUT HAUNTED EGGS UNDER A TURKEY TREE.

JOKE 142

Q: HOW OFTEN SHOULD YOU TELL CHEMISTRY JOKES?

A: PERIODICALLY.

JOKE 143

Q: WHERE IS THE BEST PLACE TO GROW PLANTS IN SCHOOL?

A: IN THE KINDER-GARDEN.

JOKE 144

Q: WHAT IS THE FASTEST WAY TO DETERMINE THE SEX OF A CHROMOSOME?

A: PULL DOWN ITS GENES.

JOKE 145

Q: WHY DOESN'T ANYONE TALK TO PI?

A: BECAUSE SHE'LL GO ON AND ON FOR ETERNITY.

JOKE 146

Q: WHAT DOES A PROUD COMPUTER CALL HIS LITTLE SON?

A: A MICROCHIP OFF THE OLD BLOCK.

JOKE 147

Q: WHY DID SUZIE SLEEP WITH A RULER?

A: TO SEE HOW LONG SHE SLEPT.

JOKE 148

Q: WHAT IS THE FIRST DERIVATIVE OF A COW?

A: PRIME RIB.

JOKE 149

Q: WHY WAS THE GEOMETRY TEACHER ABSENT?

A: SHE SPRAINED HER ANGLE.

JOKE 150

Q: WHAT DO YOU GET IF YOU CROSS A MATH TEACHER AND A WATCH?

A: ARITHMA-TICKS.

JOKE 151

Q: WHY DIDN'T THE JANITOR SHOW UP TO SCHOOL?

A: SHE KICKED THE BUCKET.

JOKE 152

Q: WHAT IS A BIRD'S FAVORITE TYPE OF MATH?

A: OWL-GEBRA.

JOKE 153

Q: WHY DID THE STUDENT TAKE A LADDER TO SCHOOL?

A: IT WAS HER FIRST DAY OF HIGH SCHOOL.

JOKE 154

Q: WHY DID THE TEACHER INSTALL LED LIGHTS?

A: BECAUSE THE CLASS WAS SO DIM.

JOKE 155

Q: WHAT DO ENGLISH TEACHERS CALL A HANGOVER?

A: THE WRATH OF GRAPES.

JOKE 156

Q: WHAT IS THE SCARIEST THING A KID CAN DRESS UP AS FOR HALLOWEEN?

A: INSTEAD OF A COSTUME, THEY GO DOOR TO DOOR WITH A FUNDRAISING PACKET.

JOKE 157

Q: WHY DOES EVERYONE HIT ON THE GEOMETRY TEACHER?

A: HE HAS ACUTE ANGLES.

JOKE 158

NOT ALL MATH PUNS ARE BAD. JUST SUM.

JOKE 159

Q: WHAT DID THE TEACHER DO WITH HER STUDENTS' ESSAYS ON THE HISTORY OF CHEESE?

A: SHE GRADED THEM.

JOKE 160

Q: DON'T BELIEVE BOOKS SAVE LIVES?

A: DINOSAURS DIDN'T READ. NOW THEY'RE EXTINCT.

JOKE 161

Q: WHAT IS A PIRATE'S FAVORITE SUBJECT?

A: AAAART

JOKE 162

Q: WHY DO STUDENTS HATE JOKES ABOUT PROM?

A: THE PUNCH LINE IS ALWAYS TOO LONG.

JOKE 163

Q: WHY DID THE RUN-ON SENTENCE THINK IT WAS PREGNANT?

A: ITS PERIOD WAS LATE.

JOKE 164

Q: WHAT DO YOU CALL A MICROBIOLOGIST WHO HAS TRAVERSED ALL 7 CONTINENTS AND SPEAKS 8 LANGUAGES?

A: A MAN OF MANY CULTURES.

JOKE 165

Q: WHAT IS THE SCHOOL VERSION OF THE MANNEQUIN CHALLENGE?

A: WHEN YOU ASK THE CLASS A QUESTION AND NO ONE HAS DONE THE READING.

JOKE 166

Q: WHY DON'T FARTS GO TO COLLEGE?

A: BECAUSE THEY ALWAYS GET EXPELLED.

JOKE 167

Q: WHAT HAPPENED WHEN THE PRINCIPAL TIED EVERYONE'S LACES TOGETHER?

A: THEY WENT ON A CLASS TRIP.

JOKE 168

Q: WHY DID THE TEACHER TURN INTO A SKELETON?

A: SHE WAITED FOR THE CLASS TO QUIET ON ITS OWN.

JOKE 169

Q: WHAT MAKES A CYCLOPS SUCH AN EFFECTIVE TEACHER?

A: HE HAS ONLY ONE PUPIL.

JOKE 170

Q: WHY DID THE CORN MAZE GO BACK TO COLLEGE?

A: IT WAS TIRED OF WORKING IN A DEAD-END FIELD.

JOKE 171

Q: WHY DID THE PIONEERS CROSS AMERICA IN COVERED WAGONS?

A: THEY DIDN'T WANT TO WAIT 40 YEARS FOR A TRAIN!

JOKE 172

Q: ANYONE KNOW ANY JOKES ABOUT SODIUM?

A: NA.

JOKE 173

Q: TEACHER: "ARE YOU SLEEPING IN MY CLASS?"

A: STUDENT: "WELL NOW I'M NOT BUT IF YOU COULD BE A LITTLE QUIETER I COULD."

JOKE 174

Q: WHAT DO MATH TEACHERS EAT ON HALLOWEEN?

A: PUMPKIN PI.

JOKE 175

Q: WHAT IS THE SECRET TO MAKING STRAIGHT A'S?

A: USE A RULER.

JOKE 176

Q: WHAT DID THE MUSTARD SAY WHEN SOMEONE OPENED THE REFRIGERATOR?

A: EXCUSE ME, I'M DRESSING.

JOKE 177

Q: HOW IS INTELLIGENCE LIKE UNDERWEAR?

A: IT'S IMPORTANT TO HAVE, BUT NOT NECESSARY TO SHOW OFF.

JOKE 178

Q: WHAT DID ONE MATH BOOK SAY TO THE OTHER?

A: DON'T BOTHER ME, I'VE GOT MY OWN PROBLEMS.

JOKE 179

Q: HOW CAN YOU TELL WHEN A TEACHER IS HUNGOVER?

A: MOVIE DAY!

JOKE 180

Q: WHAT DO YOU GET WHEN YOU MIX SULFUR, TUNGSTEN, AND SILVER?

A: SWAG

JOKE 181

Q: WHY ARE APOSTROPHES BAD DATES?

A: THEY'RE TOO POSSESSIVE.

JOKE 182

Q: WHY DO PEOPLE TELL AWFUL CHEMISTRY JOKES?

A: BECAUSE ALL THE GOOD ONES ARGON.

JOKE 183

I WENT TO THE LIBRARY TO GET A MEDICAL BOOK ON ABDOMINAL PAIN.

SOMEBODY HAD TORN THE APPENDIX OUT.

JOKE 184

Q: DID YOU HEAR ABOUT THE KIDNAPPING AT SCHOOL TODAY?

A: EVERYTHING IS FINE. HE WOKE UP.

JOKE 185

Q: DID YOU HEAR OXYGEN WENT ON A DATE WITH POTASSIUM?

A: IT WENT OK.

JOKE 186

Q: WHAT DO YOU CALL A LAUGHING JAR OF MAYONNAISE?

A: LMAYO.

JOKE 187

Q: HOW CAN YOU TELL IF YOU ARE BREAKING UP WITH AN ENGLISH TEACHER?

A: HE SAYS, "IT'S NOT YOU, IT'S I."

JOKE 188

Q: WHY IS IT SO DIFFICULT FOR PLANTS TO ESCAPE PRISON?

A: BECAUSE THEIR CELLS ARE SURROUNDED BY WALLS.

JOKE 189

Q: HOW DO YOU KNOW IF YOU'VE FAILED AN IQ TEST?

A: IF YOU PAY A WEBSITE $8.99 TO TAKE THE TEST.

JOKE 190

Q: WHY IS DIARRHEA HEREDITARY?

A: IT RUNS IN YOUR GENES!

JOKE 191

Q: WHY SHOULDN'T YOU STUDY THE PERIODIC TABLE IN ENGLISH CLASS?

A: IT'S AN ELEMENTARY MISTAKE.

JOKE 192

Q: WHAT DO ENGLISH TEACHERS LIKE TO DRINK?

A: TEQUILA MOCKINGBIRD.

JOKE 193

Q: WHAT DO YOU CALL A MUSIC TEACHER WITH ISSUES?

A: A TREBLED MAN.

JOKE 194

Q: HOW DO TEACHERS EXPLORE THE OCEAN?

A: ON A SCHOLAR-SHIP.

JOKE 195

Q: HOW WAS THE ROMAN EMPIRE DIVIDED?

A: WITH A PAIR OF CAESARS.

JOKE 196

Q: WHAT DID THE FISH SAY WHEN HE HIT THE WALL?

A: DAM!

JOKE 197

Q: MAX HAD 100 JALAPENOS. HE ATE 60 OF THEM. WHAT DOES HE HAVE NOW?

A: THE RUNS.

JOKE 198

Q: WHAT THREE CANDIES CAN YOU FIND IN EVERY SCHOOL?

A: NERDS, DUMDUMS, AND SMARTIES.

JOKE 199

Q: WHAT ROOM CAN A STUDENT NEVER ENTER?

A: A MUSHROOM.

JOKE 200

Q: WHY SHOULDN'T YOU TRUST ATOMS?

A: BECAUSE THEY MAKE UP EVERYTHING.

JOKE 201

Q: WHY WAS THE MUSIC TEACHER ARRESTED?

A: HE WAS TOO PLAYFUL WITH A MINOR.

JOKE 202

Q: WHY DID THE CHICKEN CROSS THE MOEBIUS STRIP?

A: TO GET TO THE SAME SIDE.

JOKE 203

Q: WHAT TYPE OF TREE CAN ENGLISH TEACHERS CLIMB?

A: POETRY.

JOKE 204

Q: TEACHER: "DID YOU KNOW PROTONS HAVE MASS?"

A: STUDENT: "I DIDN'T EVEN KNOW PROTONS WERE CATHOLIC."

JOKE 205

Q: WHAT DID THE GHOST TEACHER SAY TO HER CLASS?

A: LOOK AT THE BOARD AND I'LL GO THROUGH IT AGAIN.

JOKE 206

Q: WHAT'S A TORNADO'S FAVORITE GAME?

A: TWISTER.

JOKE 207

Q: WHAT DO AUSTRALIANS NEED TO GET A JOB?

A: KOALAFICATIONS.

JOKE 208

Q: TEACHER: "WHICH BOOK HAS HELPED YOU THE MOST IN YOUR LIFE?"

A: STUDENT: "MY FATHER'S CHECK BOOK!"

JOKE 209

Q: WHAT HAPPENS IF THE AVERAGE NUMBER OF BULLIES AT SCHOOL RISES?

A: THE MEAN INCREASES.

JOKE 210

Q: WHY CAN'T YOU BURY A MAN LIVING EAST OF THE MISSISSIPPI IN A GRAVE WEST OF THE MISSISSIPPI?

A: HE'S STILL ALIVE.

JOKE 211

Q: WHAT SCHOOL DO YOU GREET PEOPLE IN?

A: HI SCHOOL!

JOKE 212

DOES IT COUNT AS DIFFERENTIATED INSTRUCTION IF THE WORKSHEETS ARE PRINTED IN DIFFERENT COLORS?

JOKE 213

Q: WHAT DO BUTTERFLIES LEARN AT SCHOOL?

A: MOTHEMATICS.

JOKE 214

Q: WHY WAS THE TEACHER HAPPY AT THE HALLOWEEN PARTY?

A: BECAUSE HALLOWEEN DIDN'T FALL ON A WEDNESDAY.

JOKE 215

Q: TEACHER: "WHY HAVE YOU NOT TURNED IN YOUR HOMEWORK?"

A: STUDENT: "I MADE IT INTO A PAPER PLANE, AND SOMEONE HIJACKED IT."

JOKE 216

Q: HOW CAN TEACHERS STRESS OUT THEIR STUDENTS?

A: MAKE ALL THE ANSWERS TO A TEST, "C".

JOKE 217

Q: HOW DO YOU FIND A MATH TUTOR?

A: PLACE AN ADD.

JOKE 218

Q: WHY DID KARL MARX DISLIKE EARL GREY TEA?

A: BECAUSE ALL PROPER TEA IS THEFT.

JOKE 219

Q: HOW DOES A SQUID FIGHT ITS ENEMIES?

A: WELL ARMED.

JOKE 220

Q: HOW DO YOU WARM UP IN A SQUARE ROOM?

A: GO TO THE CORNER, WHERE IT IS ALWAYS 90 DEGREES.

JOKE 221

Q: WHAT STARTS WITH A T, ENDS WITH A T AND IS FULL OF T?

A: A TEAPOT.

JOKE 222

Q: WHAT DO YOU CALL A DINOSAUR WITH STELLAR VOCABULARY?

A: THE THESAURUS.

JOKE 223

Q: WHY DID THE MUSHROOM HATE GOING TO SCHOOL?

A: BECAUSE HE WAS ALWAYS SO SPORED.

JOKE 224

Q: WHAT DO YOU GET WHEN YOU CROSS A COMPUTER SCIENTIST WITH A WRITER?

A: A PROGRAMMAR.

JOKE 225

Q: WHY DOES THE PRINCIPAL KEEP TALKING TO ME ABOUT HAVING MORE "ARTY EYE"?

A: I TEACH READING, NOT ART.

JOKE 226

Q: HOW DO THEY TEACH LOCOMOTIVE DRIVERS?

A: THEY TRAIN THEM.

JOKE 227

Q: WHAT'S A TEACHER'S FAVORITE NATION?

A: EXPLA-NATION.

JOKE 228

Q: STUDENT: "WHEN AM I EVER GOING TO USE THIS?"

A: TEACHER: "YOU WON'T, BUT ONE OF THE SMART KIDS MIGHT."

JOKE 229

Q: WHAT FLIES AROUND GRADE SCHOOL AT NIGHT?

A: THE ALPHA-BAT.

JOKE 230

Q: WHAT DID THE WISE MAN ONCE SAY?

A: NOTHING, HE JUST LISTENED.

JOKE 231

Q: WHAT IS A TEACHER'S DAY OF REST?

A: THE REST OF LAUNDRY, THE REST OF CHORES, THE REST OF GRADING PAPERS.

JOKE 232

Q: WHAT IS THE RECIPE FOR EDITING AN ESSAY?

A: USE A LOT OF SHORTENING.

JOKE 233

Q: WHY DID THE TEACHER WRITE THE LESSON ON THE WINDOW?

A: SHE WANTED THE MATERIAL TO BE CLEAR.

JOKE 234

Q: WHAT DID THE POLICE OFFICER SAY TO HIS BELLY BUTTON?

A: YOU'RE UNDER A VEST!

JOKE 235

Q: WHAT DO YOU CALL AN ACID WITH ANGER ISSUES?

A: A-MEAN-OH ACID.

JOKE 236

Q: WHAT DO YOU CALL AN EDUCATOR WHO REFUSES TO FART IN PUBLIC?

A: A PRIVATE TOOTER.

JOKE 237

Q: WHAT DO YOU CALL THE LEADER OF A BIOLOGY GANG?

A: THE NUCLEUS

JOKE 238

Q: WHAT IS A MATH TEACHER'S FAVORITE TYPE OF TREE?

A: GEOMETRY.

JOKE 239

Q: WHAT DOES THE MAN ON THE MOON DO WHEN HIS BEARD GETS TOO LONG?

A: ECLIPSE IT!

JOKE 240

Q: WHY DIDN'T THE QUARTER ROLL DOWN THE HILL WITH THE NICKEL?

A: BECAUSE IT HAD MORE CENTS.

JOKE 241

Q: HOW MANY BIOLOGISTS DOES IT TAKE TO CHANGE A LIGHT BULB?

A: FOUR. ONE TO CHANGE IT AND THREE TO WRITE THE ENVIRONMENTAL-IMPACT STATEMENT.

JOKE 242

Q: WHY DID THE TEACHER ELOPE WITH THE JANITOR?

A: BECAUSE HE SWEPT HER OFF HER FEET.

JOKE 243

Q: IF H_2O IS THE FORMULA FOR WATER, WHAT IS THE FORMULA FOR ICE?

A: H_2O CUBED.

JOKE 244

Q: WHY DO VAMPIRES SEEM SICK?

A: THEY'RE ALWAYS COFFIN.

JOKE 245

Q: HOW DO ELEMENTARY KIDS MAKE WALLS DANCE?

A: THEY PUT SOME BOOGIE IN IT!

JOKE 246

Q: HOW DOES MOSES MAKE HIS COFFEE?

A: HEBREWS IT.

JOKE 247

Q: WHAT DOES AN ENGLISH TEACHER CALL SANTA'S ELVES?

A: SUBORDINATE CLAUSES.

JOKE 248

Q: WHAT IS A CROSS COUNTRY RUNNER'S FAVORITE SUBJECT?

A: JOG-RAPHY!

JOKE 249

Q: WHAT DO YOU CALL A SLICE OF BREAD WITH PERFECT GRADES?

A: AN HONOR ROLL.

JOKE 250

Q: WHAT DO PARALLEL LINES AND VEGANS HAVE IN COMMON?

A: THEY NEVER MEAT.

JOKE 251

Q: WHY CAN'T A NOSE BE 12 INCHES LONG?

A: BECAUSE THEN IT WOULD BE A FOOT.

JOKE 252

Q: WHAT IS THE RESULT WHEN YOU POUR ROOT BEER INTO A SQUARE GLASS?

A: BEER.

JOKE 253

Q: HOW DO YOU ASSESS WHO THE BEST COMPOSER IS?

A: YOU COMPARE THEIR SCORES.

JOKE 254

Q: WHAT MEANS THE WORLD TO A SOCIAL STUDIES TEACHER?

A: A GLOBE.

JOKE 255

Q: DO YOU KNOW WHAT HAPPENED TO THE SICK CHEMISTRY TEACHER?

A: IF YOU CAN'T HELIUM, AND YOU CAN'T CURIUM, YOU'LL PROBABLY HAVE TO BARIUM.

JOKE 256

Q: WHY DID CLOSING HER EYES REMIND THE TEACHER OF HER CLASSROOM?

A: BECAUSE THERE WERE NO PUPILS TO SEE.

JOKE 257

Q: WHY DO WE CALL THE EARLY DAYS OF HISTORY THE DARK AGES?

A: BECAUSE THERE WERE SO MANY KNIGHTS.

JOKE 258

Q: HOW DO YOU ATTEND A SCHOOL FOR GHOSTS?

A: ACT SUPER NATURAL.

JOKE 259

Q: WHY DID THE ATTACKING ARMY USE ACID?

A: TO NEUTRALIZE THE ENEMY'S BASE.

JOKE 260

Q: HOW CAN YOU MAKE SEVEN EVEN?

A: TAKE AWAY THE "S".

JOKE 261

Q: WHAT DID THE BUFFALO TELL HIS SON WHEN HE LEFT FOR UNIVERSITY?

A: BISON.

JOKE 262

Q: WHAT'S A MATH TEACHER'S FAVORITE KIND OF DANCING?

A: SQUARE DANCING.

JOKE 263

Q: WHAT BEGINS AT THE END AND ENDS AT THE BEGINNING?

A: BACK TO SCHOOL ADS.

JOKE 264

Q: WHY DO MAGICIANS ACE ALL THEIR TESTS?

A: THEY'RE GOOD AT TRICK QUESTIONS.

JOKE 265

Q: TEACHER: "WHY DO YOU HAVE COTTON PLUGGED IN YOUR EARS?"

A: STUDENT: "YOU SAID THINGS GO IN ONE EAR AND OUT THE OTHER, SO I AM TRYING TO KEEP THEM ALL IN!"

JOKE 266

Q: WHAT DO YOU CALL AN ENGLISH STUDENT WHO USED TO BE ANXIOUS?

A: PAST TENSE.

JOKE 267

Q: WHAT DO YOU CALL A TEACHER WHO FORGETS TO TAKE ATTENDANCE?

A: ABSENT-MINDED.

JOKE 268

Q: WHAT WOULD YOU FIND IN CHARLES DICKENS' KITCHEN?

A: THE BEST OF THYMES, THE WORST OF THYMES.

JOKE 269

Q: WHY WAS THE STUDENT DISAPPOINTED IN HERSELF FOR FAILING HER PSYCHIC EXAM?

A: BECAUSE SHE JUST DIDN'T SEE IT COMING.

JOKE 270

Q: WHAT DO YOU DO IF YOUR STUDENTS ROLL THEIR EYES AT YOU?

A: PICK THEM UP AND ROLL THEM BACK.

JOKE 271

Q: WHAT DO YOU CALL A SINGING LAPTOP?

A: A DELL!

JOKE 272

Q: WHY WAS SCHOOL EASIER FOR CAVE PEOPLE?

A: THERE WAS NO HISTORY TO LEARN.

JOKE 273

Q: FATHER: HOW DID YOUR FIREWORKS EXAM GO?

A: SON: I PASSED WITH FLYING COLORS!

JOKE 274

Q: WHY SHOULD KIDS GO TO COLLEGE?

A: SO THEY CAN SPEND 40% OF THEIR LIVES ON CONFERENCE CALLS.

JOKE 275

Q: WHY SHOULDN'T YOU WORK IN AN ORANGE JUICE FACTORY?

A: BECAUSE YOU CAN'T CONCENTRATE.

JOKE 276

Q: HOW DID THE ELEMENTARY TEACHER QUIET HIS CLASS?

A: HE TOLD THE STUDENTS GLUE STICKS WERE LIP BALM.

JOKE 277

Q: WHY IS IT A BAD IDEA TO DO MATH IN THE JUNGLE?

A: BECAUSE IF YOU ADD 4+4 YOU GET ATE!

JOKE 278

Q: WHAT HAS GIVEN MR. BUBBLES NIGHTMARES SINCE ELEMENTARY SCHOOL?

A: POP QUIZZES!

JOKE 279

Q: WHAT HAPPENED TO THE MATH TEACHER'S GARDEN?

A: THE PLANTS ALL GREW SQUARE ROOTS.

JOKE 280

Q: WHY DID THE GIRAFFE GET BAD GRADES?

A: HE HAD HIS HEAD IN THE CLOUDS.

JOKE 281

Q: WHAT DID THE CHEERLEADER SAY WHEN SHE RECEIVED DETENTION?

A: BRING IT ON.

JOKE 282

Q: WHAT'S A MATH TEACHER'S FAVORITE SEASON?

A: SUM-MER.

JOKE 283

Q: WHY WAS THE ANGLE REFUSED A LOAN?

A: ITS PARENTS WOULDN'T COSINE.

JOKE 284

Q: HOW IS COLLEGE THE OPPOSITE OF KIDNAPPING?

A: THEY DEMAND $100,000 FROM YOU, OR THEY'LL SEND YOUR KID BACK.

JOKE 285

Q: WHY WAS THE CROSS-EYED TEACHER FIRED?

A: HE HAD NO CONTROL OVER HIS PUPILS.

JOKE 286

Q: WHY ARE BIOLOGY TEACHERS ALSO GREAT PHILOSOPHERS?

A: BECAUSE THEY GIVE GREAT LIFE LESSONS.

JOKE 287

Q: WHAT ARE THREE REASONS WHY SOMEONE WOULD BECOME A TEACHER?

A: JUNE, JULY AND AUGUST.

JOKE 288

Q: HOW ARE ENGLISH TEACHERS AND COKE DEALERS ALIKE?

A: THEY FOCUS ON THE LAST LINE.

JOKE 289

Q: GEOGRAPHY TEACHER: "DID YOU FINISH THIS BOOK ON MOUNT EVEREST?"

A: STUDENT: "IT WAS A REAL CLIFF-HANGER."

JOKE 290

Q: WHY DIDN'T THE TEACHER GRADE HER PAPERS?

A: HER PINTEREST FEED WAS FIRE.

JOKE 291

Q: WHERE WAS THE MAGNA CARTA SIGNED?

A: AT THE BOTTOM.

JOKE 292

Q: WHAT DO YOU CALL A BONE OF THE BODY THAT DEFIES CHURCH TEACHING?

A: A BLASFEMUR.

JOKE 293

Q: WHY DID THE MUSIC TEACHER NEED A LADDER?

A: TO REACH THE HIGH NOTES.

JOKE 294

Q: WHAT IS A CONCLUSION TO STUDENTS?

A: THE PART WHERE THEY GET TIRED OF THINKING.

JOKE 295

Q: WHY DID THE COMPUTER SCIENCE TEACHER QUIT?

A: SHE HAD A TERMINAL ILLNESS.

JOKE 296

Q: WHY DO STUDENTS CALL THEIR MATH TEACHER MEAN?

A: BECAUSE HE CALLED THEM AVERAGE.

JOKE 297

Q: WHAT DID ONE CELL SAY TO HIS SISTER CELL WHEN SHE STEPPED IN HIS TOE?

A: MITOSIS.

JOKE 298

Q: WHY DID THE TEACHER TOSS HER CLOCK OUT OF THE SCHOOL WINDOW?

A: SHE WANTED TIME TO FLY.

JOKE 299

Q: WHERE DO KITTENS GO ON SCHOOL TRIPS?

A: TO THE MEWSEUM.

JOKE 300

Q: DO YOU WANT TO HEAR SOMETHING ODD?

A: NUMBERS THAT CAN'T BE DIVIDED BY 2.

JOKE 301

Q: WHAT'S THE DIFFERENCE BETWEEN A CAT AND A COMMA?

A: CATS HAVE CLAWS AT THE END OF THEIR PAWS AND COMMAS ARE A PAUSE AT THE END OF A CLAUSE.

JOKE 302

Q: HOW DO SNAILS WRESTLE?

A: THEY SLUG IT OUT.

JOKE 303

Q: WHY DID THE STUDENT DO HER MATH ASSIGNMENT ON THE FLOOR?

A: THE TEACHER SAID NOT TO USE TABLES.

JOKE 304

Q: HOW DOES JULIET MAINTAIN HER BODY TEMPERATURE?

A: ROMEOSTASIS.

JOKE 305

Q: HOW MANY MEN WERE BORN IN 2012?

A: NONE, ONLY BABIES WERE BORN.

JOKE 306

Q: HOW CAN A DOCTOR TELL IF A PATIENT IS A TEACHER?

A: BY CHECKING THEIR BLADDER SIZE.

JOKE 307

Q: WHY CAN'T CATS WORK WITH COMPUTERS?

A: THEY GET TOO DISTRACTED CHASING THE MOUSE.

JOKE 308

Q: WHAT SCHOOL SUPPLY IS ALWAYS SLEEPY?

A: A KNAPSACK.

JOKE 309

Q: WHAT DO SCHOLARS SNACK ON?

A: ACADEMIA NUTS.

JOKE 310

Q: WHY ARE WRITERS ALWAYS COLD?

A: THEY'RE SURROUNDED BY DRAFTS.

JOKE 311

Q: WHY ARE GEOGRAPHERS AMUSED BY MOUNTAINS?

A: BECAUSE THEY ARE HILL AREAS.

JOKE 312

Q: HOW DOES A BACKWARDS POET WRITE?

A: INVERSE.

JOKE 313

Q: WHY DID THE TEACHER WEAR SUNGLASSES DURING CLASS?

A: BECAUSE HIS STUDENTS WERE SO BRIGHT.

JOKE 314

Q: WHERE DO HIPPOS GO TO COLLEGE?

A: HIPPOCAMPUS.

JOKE 315

Q: IF I HAVE 6 BOTTLES IN ONE HAND AND 7 IN THE OTHER HAND, WHAT DO I HAVE?

A: A DRINKING PROBLEM.

JOKE 316

Q: WHY WAS THE NUMBER 4 KICKED OUT OF THE CLUB?

A: FOR BEING 2 SQUARE.

JOKE 317

Q: WHY IS TIME A GREAT TEACHER?

A: IT EVENTUALLY KILLS ALL ITS STUDENTS.

JOKE 318

Q: WHY DO PEOPLE HATE RUSSIAN DOLLS?

A: BECAUSE THEY ARE SO FULL OF THEMSELVES.

JOKE 319

Q: WHY DON'T SHEPHERDS LEARN TO COUNT?

A: BECAUSE IF THEY DID, THEY WOULD ALWAYS BE DOZING OFF.

JOKE 320

Q: WHAT DID THE PASSIVE-AGGRESSIVE RAVEN SAY TO EDGAR ALLEN POE?

A: "NEVERMIND."

JOKE 321

Q: WHAT KIND OF MUSIC DID THE PILGRIMS LISTEN TO?

A: PLYMOUTH ROCK.

JOKE 322

Q: WHY WERE GRADUATION SPEECHES INVENTED?

A: BECAUSE STUDENTS SHOULDN'T BE RELEASED INTO SOCIETY UNTIL THEY HAVE BEEN SUFFICIENTLY SEDATED.

JOKE 323

Q: WHY ARE CHROMOSOMES FEATURED IN COMMERCIALS?

A: BECAUSE SEX CELLS.

JOKE 324

Q: WHAT DO YOU CALL AN EDUCATED TUBE?

A: A GRADUATED CYLINDER.

JOKE 325

Q: WHY WAS THE FRACTION NERVOUS TO MARRY THE DECIMAL?

A: BECAUSE HE WOULD NEED TO CONVERT.

JOKE 326

Q: WHY DO TEACHERS AVOID THEIR STUDENTS IN PUBLIC?

A: SO THEY CAN WEAR THE SAME OUTFIT TO SCHOOL.

JOKE 327

Q: WHAT DO YOU SAY TO SOOTHE AN ENGLISH TEACHER?

A: THEY'RE, THERE, THEIR.

JOKE 328

Q: WHY DOES NOBODY TALK TO CIRCLES?

A: BECAUSE THERE'S NO POINT.

JOKE 329

Q: WHAT MAKES SOMEONE WELL-READ?

A: READING WHILE SUNBATHING.

JOKE 330

Q: WHAT DO CARS LIKE TO READ ABOUT?

A: AUTOBIOGRAPHIES.

Printed in Great Britain
by Amazon